MW01171586

Published by Winn Publications, Melbourne, Florida, winnpublications.com

ISBN: 979-8-9897876-9-2

SHEDDING POUNDS, GAINING PURPOSE:
THE
WEIGHTY JOY
OF
SURRENDER
WORKBOOK

CALEB JAKES

INTRODUCTION

Welcome to a transformative journey designed to deepen your understanding and practice of spiritual living. This workbook guides you through key themes of joy, faith, and personal growth. Begin with the **Genesis of Joy**, where you'll explore the essence of joy and its origins in your life. This sets the foundation for what follows. In **Who Told You That?**, challenge and reconsider the beliefs that shape your worldview and identify which ones serve your spiritual growth. **Nourishing the Spirit** dives into practices that enrich your inner life, ensuring your spirit is well-fed through daily routines and reflections.

Reflect on the influence of close relationships in **Who Is in Your Top 5** and their impact on your spiritual and emotional well-being. **Faith in the Digital World** addresses the challenges and opportunities of maintaining faith in an era dominated by digital interactions. In **Embracing Divine Uniqueness**, break free from the comparison trap and celebrate your unique spiritual journey and identity. **Gratitude: The Heartbeat of Joy** encourages cultivating a habit of gratitude, fundamental to perceiving and multiplying the joys in your life.

Explore forgiveness as a path to healing and spiritual renewal in **The Transformative Power of Forgiving**. Discover the joy and spiritual fulfillment that comes from serving others in **The Art of Serving Others**. Conclude your journey in **Stepping into Joyionaire Status**, which celebrates your transformation and the realization of your highest spiritual potential, guiding you to live as a Joyionaire.

Each chapter is accompanied by thoughtful questions and exercises that encourage reflection, writing, and action on the spiritual principles discussed. By engaging with these materials, you will gain insights into your spiritual life and develop habits that lead to lasting joy and fulfillment. Prepare to engage deeply, reflect honestly, and embrace the journey to becoming a more spiritually enriched individual.

Brief Checklist for Spiritual Wellness

Rate each statement based on your recent feelings and behaviors. Circle your number 1(rarely) to 5(always)

Daily Spiritual Practices:
Do I engage in daily prayer or meditation?

1   2   3   4   5

Do I set aside time for spiritual reading or study?

1   2   3   4   5

Mindfulness:
Am I regularly practicing mindfulness in my daily activities?

1   2   3   4   5

Do I maintain a moment-to-moment awareness of my thoughts and feelings?

1   2   3   4   5

Gratitude:
Do I maintain a daily gratitude journal or take time to reflect on what I am thankful for?

1   2   3   4   5

Community Interaction:
Am I actively participating in a spiritual or religious community?

1   2   3   4   5

Do I have spiritual conversations with others that enrich my understanding?

1   2   3   4   5

Personal Reflection:
Do I regularly reflect on my personal values and how they align with my actions?

1   2   3   4   5

REFLECTION

GENESIS OF JOY

What truly is joy, and where does its journey begin in our lives? The "Genesis of Joy" aims to peel back the layers of your daily experiences to uncover the essence of true happiness. Like detectives on a quest, we dive into the simplicity and complexity of joy—its subtle signs, its grand moments, and its quiet presence in our everyday lives. This chapter is not just about identifying joy but understanding its roots and how it intertwines with the fabric of our being. It's about recognizing joy in the places we least expect—within a morning's quiet, the laughter shared with a friend or the peace of a setting sun. Let's rediscover together the foundational sparks of joy that light up our world.

Nehemiah 8:10 - "The joy of the Lord is your strength."

REFLECT ON A TIME WHEN JOY FELT MOST ALIVE IN YOUR HEART. WHAT WERE THE ELEMENTS OF THAT MOMENT, AND HOW CAN YOU INTEGRATE THEM INTO YOUR DAILY LIFE?

Nehemiah 8:10 - "The joy of the Lord is your strength."

CONSIDER THE BARRIERS THAT HAVE HISTORICALLY PREVENTED YOU FROM EXPERIENCING JOY. HOW CAN YOU BEGIN DISMANTLING THESE BARRIERS TODAY?

Nehemiah 8:10 - "The joy of the Lord is your strength."

JOY OFTEN COMES IN SIMPLE FORMS. WHAT SIMPLE PLEASURES BRING YOU THE MOST JOY, AND HOW CAN YOU MAKE THEM A REGULAR PART OF YOUR LIFE?

Nehemiah 8:10 - "The joy of the Lord is your strength."

HOW HAS YOUR DEFINITION OF JOY EVOLVED, AND WHAT LIFE LESSONS CONTRIBUTED TO THIS EVOLUTION?

Nehemiah 8:10 - "The joy of the Lord is your strength."

IDENTIFY A MOMENT WHEN YOU FOUND JOY IN A CHALLENGING SITUATION. WHAT DID THIS EXPERIENCE TEACH YOU ABOUT THE NATURE OF JOY?

FREE SPACE

CHAPTER TAKEAWAYS

Date:

_____

_____

_____

_____

_____

_____

_____

_____

_____

_____

_____

WHO TOLD YOU THAT?

So many of us carry around beliefs that weigh us down—ideas about not being good enough, not fitting in, or not deserving happiness. "Who Told You That?" is a chapter dedicated to uncovering the roots of these negative beliefs about ourselves. Where did these thoughts come from? Were they whispered to us in moments of doubt, or did they grow from comparisons and criticisms? This chapter invites you on a journey to challenge and change these harmful narratives. It's about questioning the origin of our self-limiting beliefs to break free from them. Through reflection and inquiry, we aim to replace these negative voices with a kinder, truer dialogue that speaks to our strengths and potential. Let's embark on a path to uncover and affirm our truths, fostering a more joyful and authentic self-view.

Romans 12:2 - "Do not conform to the pattern of this world, but be transformed by the renewing of your mind"

RECALL A BELIEF YOU HELD ABOUT YOURSELF THAT LIMITED YOUR POTENTIAL. WHERE DID THIS BELIEF COME FROM, AND HOW HAVE YOU CHALLENGED IT?

Romans 12:2 - "Do not conform to the pattern of this world, but be transformed by the renewing of your mind"

HOW DO SOCIETAL EXPECTATIONS INFLUENCE YOUR PERCEPTION OF YOURSELF AND YOUR ABILITIES? REFLECT ON A TIME WHEN YOU OVERCAME THESE EXTERNAL PRESSURES.

Romans 12:2 - "Do not conform to the pattern of this world, but be transformed by the renewing of your mind"

THINK OF A PIECE OF ADVICE YOU ONCE RECEIVED THAT TRANSFORMED YOUR OUTLOOK. WHO GAVE YOU THIS ADVICE, AND WHY WAS IT SO IMPACTFUL?

Romans 12:2 - "Do not conform to the pattern of this world, but be transformed by the renewing of your mind"

CONSIDER THE NARRATIVES YOU'VE BEEN TOLD ABOUT SUCCESS AND FAILURE. HOW HAVE THESE NARRATIVES SHAPED YOUR ACTIONS, AND HOW DO YOU WISH TO REWRITE THEM?

Romans 12:2 - "Do not conform to the pattern of this world, but be transformed by the renewing of your mind"

REFLECT ON A LIE YOU ONCE BELIEVED ABOUT YOUR CAPABILITIES. HOW DID YOU UNCOVER THE TRUTH, AND WHAT IMPACT DID THIS REVELATION HAVE ON YOUR LIFE?

FREE SPACE

CHAPTER TAKEAWAYS

Date:

NOURISHING THE SPIRIT

Just as our bodies crave nourishment, so does our spirit—a vital ingredient for cultivating joy. "Nourishing the Spirit" delves into the myriad ways we can feed our souls and enrich our lives with a lasting sense of fulfillment. From the tranquility of nature to the warmth of human connection, this chapter reveals the simple yet profound acts that replenish our inner selves. Among these practices, gratitude stands out as a powerful sustainer of the spirit. It teaches us to appreciate the abundance within and around us, transforming ordinary moments into sources of joy. This chapter invites you to identify what spiritually sustains you, including the practice of gratitude and encourages habits that connect you to a deeper sense of purpose and joy. As we journey through these pages, let's embrace the rituals that keep our spirits vibrant and our heart's content, with gratitude leading the way.

Romans 12:2 - "Do not conform to the pattern of this world, but be transformed by the renewing of your mind"

WHAT SPIRITUAL PRACTICES BRING YOU PEACE AND WHY? HOW CAN YOU MAKE THEM A MORE PROMINENT PART OF YOUR DAILY ROUTINE?

Romans 12:2 - "Do not conform to the pattern of this world, but be transformed by the renewing of your mind"

IN MOMENTS OF SPIRITUAL DROUGHT, WHAT RESOURCES OR ACTIVITIES HELP REPLENISH YOUR SPIRIT?

Romans 12:2 - "Do not conform to the pattern of this world, but be transformed by the renewing of your mind"

REFLECT ON A TIME WHEN YOUR SPIRIT FELT FULLY NOURISHED. WHAT WERE YOU DOING, AND HOW CAN YOU REPLICATE THAT FEELING?

Romans 12:2 - "Do not conform to the pattern of this world, but be transformed by the renewing of your mind"

HOW DOES THE COMPANY YOU KEEP AFFECT YOUR SPIRITUAL WELL-BEING? DESCRIBE STEPS YOU CAN TAKE TO SURROUND YOURSELF WITH MORE POSITIVE INFLUENCES.

Romans 12:2 - "Do not conform to the pattern of this world, but be transformed by the renewing of your mind"

WHAT ROLE DOES GRATITUDE PLAY IN NOURISHING YOUR SPIRIT? LIST FIVE THINGS YOU'RE DEEPLY GRATEFUL FOR AND WHY.

FREE SPACE

CHAPTER TAKEAWAYS

Date:

_____

_____

_____

_____

_____

_____

_____

_____

_____

_____

_____

WHO IS IN YOUR TOP 5?

The people we choose to surround ourselves with have a profound impact on our happiness. "Who Is in Your Top 5?" encourages you to take a closer look at your closest relationships and their influence on your sense of joy. This chapter explores the dynamics of social connections, stressing the importance of fostering bonds that lift us up and bring positivity into our lives. It's a chance to examine the energy we exchange in these relationships and make mindful decisions to invest in those who truly enhance our well-being. Moreover, one of the intriguing aspects we'll tackle is the idea of expanding your circle—considering who might become a valuable addition to your "Top 6." This discussion opens up the possibility of welcoming new sources of strength, laughter, and shared joy into your life. Together, let's discover how expanding our circle can enrich our journey toward happiness.

Proverbs 13:20 - - "Walk with the wise and become wise, for a companion of fools suffers harm."

IDENTIFY FIVE PEOPLE WHO POSITIVELY INFLUENCE YOUR GROWTH. WHAT UNIQUE QUALITIES DOES EACH PERSON BRING TO YOUR LIFE?

_____

_____

_____

_____

_____

_____

_____

_____

_____

_____

_____

_____

_____

_____

_____

Proverbs 13:20 - - "Walk with the wise and become wise, for a companion of fools suffers harm."

REFLECT ON THE ENERGY AND CONVERSATIONS YOU SHARE WITH YOUR TOP FIVE. HOW DO THEY CONTRIBUTE TO YOUR PURPOSE AND JOY?

Proverbs 13:20 - - "Walk with the wise and become wise, for a companion of fools suffers harm."

HOW DO YOU NOURISH THE RELATIONSHIPS WITH THOSE IN YOUR TOP FIVE, AND HOW CAN YOU DEEPEN THESE CONNECTIONS?

Proverbs 13:20 - - "Walk with the wise and become wise, for a companion of fools suffers harm."

THINK ABOUT A PERSON YOU ADMIRE OUTSIDE OF YOUR IMMEDIATE CIRCLE. WHAT STEPS CAN YOU TAKE TO LEARN FROM OR INCLUDE THEM IN YOUR CIRCLE?

Proverbs 13:20 - - "Walk with the wise and become wise, for a companion of fools suffers harm."

CONSIDER THE DIVERSITY WITHIN YOUR TOP FIVE. HOW DO THE DIFFERENT PERSPECTIVES AND LIFE EXPERIENCES ENRICH YOUR PERSONAL GROWTH?

_____

_____

_____

_____

_____

_____

_____

_____

_____

_____

_____

_____

_____

_____

FREE SPACE

CHAPTER TAKEAWAYS

Date:

FAITH IN THE DIGITAL WORLD

Maintaining faith and joy in a digitally dominated era presents unique challenges and opportunities. "Faith in the Digital World" navigates the complexities of online life, seeking balance in an environment that can often feel overwhelming. This chapter offers strategies for using digital tools to enhance rather than diminish your spiritual journey, highlighting the importance of mindful consumption and meaningful connections. It's about finding harmony between our online and offline selves, ensuring that our digital experiences contribute positively to our overall sense of joy and fulfillment.

Philippians 4:8 - "Finally, brothers and sisters, whatever is true, whatever is noble, whatever is right, whatever is pure, whatever is lovely, whatever is admirable—if anything is excellent or praiseworthy —think about such things."

IN WHAT WAYS HAS THE DIGITAL WORLD STRENGTHENED YOUR FAITH, AND HOW DO YOU NAVIGATE THE CHALLENGES IT PRESENTS TO YOUR SPIRITUAL JOURNEY?

Philippians 4:8 - "Finally, brothers and sisters, whatever is true, whatever is noble, whatever is right, whatever is pure, whatever is lovely, whatever is admirable—if anything is excellent or praiseworthy —think about such things."

REFLECT ON A DIGITAL ENCOUNTER (BE IT A VIDEO, ARTICLE, OR SOCIAL MEDIA POST) THAT PROFOUNDLY IMPACTED YOUR FAITH. WHAT WAS ITS MESSAGE, AND WHY DID IT RESONATE WITH YOU?

Philippians 4:8 - "Finally, brothers and sisters, whatever is true, whatever is noble, whatever is right, whatever is pure, whatever is lovely, whatever is admirable—if anything is excellent or praiseworthy —think about such things."

CONSIDER THE BALANCE BETWEEN DIGITAL CONNECTION AND SPIRITUAL SOLITUDE. HOW DO YOU FIND HARMONY BETWEEN THESE IN YOUR FAITH PRACTICE?

Philippians 4:8 - "Finally, brothers and sisters, whatever is true, whatever is noble, whatever is right, whatever is pure, whatever is lovely, whatever is admirable—if anything is excellent or praiseworthy —think about such things."

HOW DO YOU USE DIGITAL PLATFORMS TO SPREAD JOY AND FAITH, AND WHAT GUIDELINES DO YOU SET FOR YOURSELF TO MAINTAIN AUTHENTICITY AND INTEGRITY ONLINE?

Philippians 4:8 - "Finally, brothers and sisters, whatever is true, whatever is noble, whatever is right, whatever is pure, whatever is lovely, whatever is admirable—if anything is excellent or praiseworthy —think about such things."

DISCUSS THE ROLE OF DIGITAL COMMUNITIES IN YOUR SPIRITUAL GROWTH. HOW DO YOU ENSURE THESE SPACES ENHANCE RATHER THAN DETRACT FROM YOUR FAITH?

FREE SPACE

CHAPTER TAKEAWAYS

Date:

_____

_____

_____

_____

_____

_____

_____

_____

_____

_____

_____

EMBRACING DIVINE UNIQUENESS: KILLING THE COMPARISON TRAP

In the age of social media, where comparison is a constant, embracing our unique journey is crucial. 'Embracing Divine Uniqueness' invites you to move beyond social media's comparison trap and celebrate your individuality. This chapter is a call to break free from the shadows of comparison, which undermine our self-worth, and to cherish the unique beauty of our paths. It encourages honoring your talents and experiences, asserting that real happiness stems from authenticity. By valuing our differences, we affirm our self-worth and open our hearts to true joy—joy that is sincerely ours. Let's disconnect our self-esteem from social media's approval and find value in our own stories.

Psalm 139:14 - "I praise you because I am fearfully and wonderfully made; your works are wonderful, I know that full well."

REFLECT ON A TIME COMPARISON THAT DIMINISHED YOUR SENSE OF SELF-WORTH. HOW DID YOU REGAIN PERSPECTIVE AND APPRECIATION FOR YOUR JOURNEY?

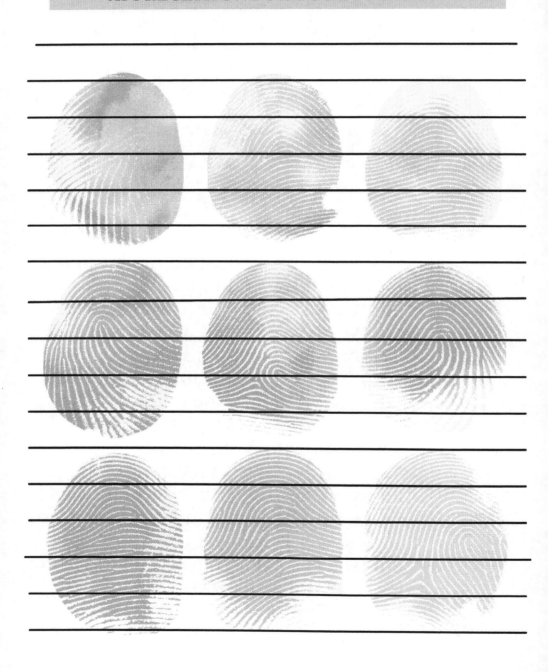

Psalm 139:14 - "I praise you because I am fearfully and wonderfully made; your works are wonderful, I know that full well."

HOW DOES SOCIAL MEDIA INFLUENCE YOUR TENDENCY TO COMPARE? COMMIT TO ONE ACTION THAT WILL HELP REDUCE NEGATIVE COMPARISONS.

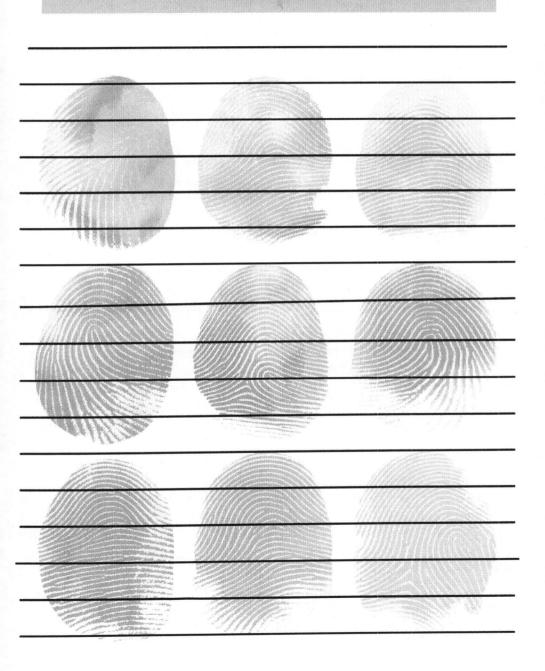

Psalm 139:14 - "I praise you because I am fearfully and wonderfully made; your works are wonderful, I know that full well."

IDENTIFY THE AREAS OF LIFE WHERE YOU'RE MOST SUSCEPTIBLE TO COMPARISON. WHAT UNIQUE QUALITIES DO YOU POSSESS THAT YOU SHOULD CELEBRATE INSTEAD?

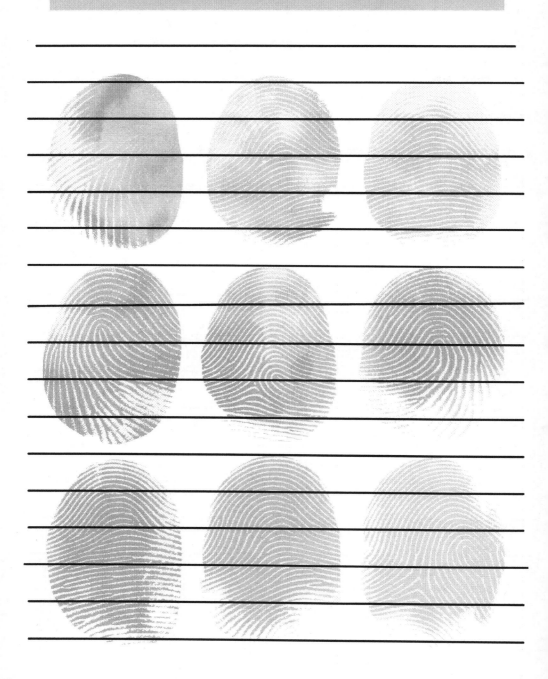

Psalm 139:14 - "I praise you because I am fearfully and wonderfully made; your works are wonderful, I know that full well."

CONSIDER THE POSITIVE ASPECTS OF COMPARISON. HAVE THERE BEEN INSTANCES WHERE COMPARISON MOTIVATED YOU POSITIVELY, AND HOW CAN YOU HARNESS THIS CONSTRUCTIVELY?

Psalm 139:14 - "I praise you because I am fearfully and wonderfully made; your works are wonderful, I know that full well."

REFLECT ON THE ROLE OF EMPATHY IN OVERCOMING THE COMPARISON TRAP. HOW CAN UNDERSTANDING OTHERS' STRUGGLES AND SUCCESSES HELP MITIGATE ENVY?

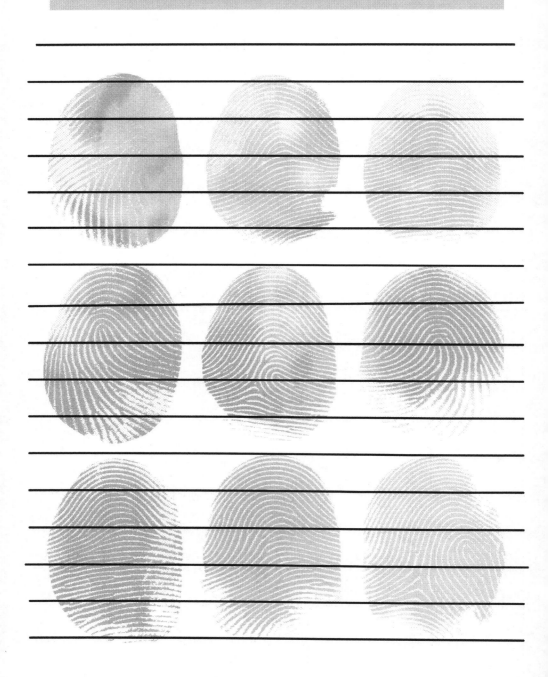

FREE SPACE

CHAPTER TAKEAWAYS

Date:

_____

_____

_____

_____

_____

_____

_____

_____

_____

_____

_____

GRATITUDE: THE HEARTBEAT OF JOY

Gratitude is the pulse that keeps the heart of joy beating. "Gratitude: The Heartbeat of Joy" explores the transformative power of thankfulness in cultivating a happier, more content life. This chapter invites you to practice gratitude in daily moments, big and small, and witness its profound impact on your outlook. By turning our attention to what we have, rather than what we lack, we unlock a deeper appreciation for life and all its gifts. Join us in nurturing a grateful heart, and let's watch as it becomes a wellspring of joy.

1 Thessalonians 5:16-18 - "Rejoice always, pray continually, give thanks in all circumstances; for this is God's will for you in Christ Jesus."

REFLECT DEEPLY ON AN ORDINARY MOMENT THAT FILLED YOU WITH GRATITUDE. WHAT DETAILS MADE THIS MOMENT MEMORABLE?

1 Thessalonians 5:16-18 - "Rejoice always, pray continually, give thanks in all circumstances; for this is God's will for you in Christ Jesus."

GRATITUDE CAN TRANSFORM PERSPECTIVE. DESCRIBE A DIFFICULT SITUATION WHERE FINDING GRATITUDE CHANGED YOUR OUTLOOK.

1 Thessalonians 5:16-18 - "Rejoice always, pray continually, give thanks in all circumstances; for this is God's will for you in Christ Jesus."

HOW DOES EXPRESSING GRATITUDE TOWARDS OTHERS ENHANCE YOUR SENSE OF JOY AND PURPOSE?

1 Thessalonians 5:16-18 - "Rejoice always, pray continually, give thanks in all circumstances; for this is God's will for you in Christ Jesus."

ENVISION YOUR LIFE ONE YEAR FROM NOW, FULLY INFUSED WITH GRATITUDE. WHAT CHANGES DO YOU SEE, AND HOW DOES IT AFFECT YOUR DAILY LIVING?

1 Thessalonians 5:16-18 - "Rejoice always, pray continually, give thanks in all circumstances; for this is God's will for you in Christ Jesus."

CREATE A GRATITUDE RITUAL FOR YOUR DAILY ROUTINE. WHAT ARE FIVE THINGS YOU WILL COMMIT TO BEING GRATEFUL FOR, REGARDLESS OF CIRCUMSTANCES?

FREE SPACE

CHAPTER TAKEAWAYS

Date:

_____

_____

_____

_____

_____

_____

_____

_____

_____

_____

THE TRANSFORMATIVE POWER OF FORGIVING

Forgiveness can liberate the soul and open the gates to new beginnings of joy. "The Transformative Power of Forgiving" examines the challenging yet rewarding path of letting go of past grievances. This chapter is about understanding forgiveness as a gift to oneself—a key to unlocking peace and happiness that resentment has kept at bay. Through stories and reflections, we'll explore the journey of forgiveness, not just as an act of compassion towards others, but as a profound act of self-love and healing.

Colossians 3:13 - "Bear with each other and forgive one another if any of you has a grievance against someone. Forgive as the Lord forgave you."

RECALL A MOMENT WHEN FORGIVING SOMEONE FREED YOU FROM CARRYING THE WEIGHT OF RESENTMENT. HOW DID THIS ACT OF FORGIVENESS CHANGE YOU?

Colossians 3:13 - "Bear with each other and forgive one another if any of you has a grievance against someone. Forgive as the Lord forgave you."

FORGIVENESS IS OFTEN A JOURNEY RATHER THAN A SINGLE ACT. DESCRIBE A TIME WHEN YOU STRUGGLED TO FORGIVE AND THE STEPS YOU TOOK TO EVENTUALLY FIND PEACE.

Colossians 3:13 - "Bear with each other and forgive one another if any of you has a grievance against someone. Forgive as the Lord forgave you."

HOW DOES YOUR FAITH INFLUENCE YOUR UNDERSTANDING AND PRACTICE OF FORGIVENESS, AND CAN YOU SHARE A SCRIPTURAL OR SPIRITUAL INSIGHT THAT GUIDES YOU?

Colossians 3:13 - "Bear with each other and forgive one another if any of you has a grievance against someone. Forgive as the Lord forgave you."

REFLECT ON THE RELATIONSHIP BETWEEN FORGIVENESS AND SELF-LOVE. HOW HAS FORGIVING OTHERS LED TO A DEEPER ACCEPTANCE AND LOVE FOR YOURSELF?

_____

_____

_____

_____

_____

_____

_____

_____

_____

_____

_____

_____

_____

_____

Colossians 3:13 - "Bear with each other and forgive one another if any of you has a grievance against someone. Forgive as the Lord forgave you."

FREE SPACE

CHAPTER TAKEAWAYS

Date:

_____

_____

_____

_____

_____

_____

_____

_____

_____

_____

_____

THE ART OF SERVING OTHERS

There's a unique joy that comes from giving, distinct from all other pleasures. "The Art of Serving Others" celebrates the happiness we find in selflessness and the impact of altruism on our well-being. This chapter looks at the ways serving others enriches our lives, bringing fulfillment and joy that selfish pursuits cannot match. By shining a light on the beauty of generosity and compassion, we encourage a life oriented towards giving—finding in it the essence of true joy.

Galatians 5:13 - "You, my brothers and sisters, were called to be free. But do not use your freedom to indulge the flesh; rather, serve one another humbly in love."

SHARE AN EXPERIENCE WHERE SERVING OTHERS UNEXPECTEDLY ENRICHED YOUR OWN LIFE. WHAT DID YOU LEARN ABOUT JOY AND PURPOSE THROUGH THIS ACT OF SERVICE?

Galatians 5:13 - "You, my brothers and sisters, were called to be free. But do not use your freedom to indulge the flesh; rather, serve one another humbly in love."

HOW DOES SERVING OTHERS REFLECT YOUR FAITH AND VALUES, AND HOW DO YOU FIND OPPORTUNITIES TO SERVE IN YOUR DAILY LIFE?

Galatians 5:13 - "You, my brothers and sisters, were called to be free. But do not use your freedom to indulge the flesh; rather, serve one another humbly in love."

REFLECT ON A TIME WHEN SERVING SOMEONE WAS PARTICULARLY CHALLENGING. WHAT OBSTACLES DID YOU FACE, AND HOW DID YOU OVERCOME THEM?

Galatians 5:13 - "You, my brothers and sisters, were called to be free. But do not use your freedom to indulge the flesh; rather, serve one another humbly in love."

SERVING OTHERS CAN TAKE MANY FORMS. DESCRIBE A UNIQUE WAY YOU'VE BEEN ABLE TO SERVE THAT ALIGNS WITH YOUR TALENTS AND PASSIONS.

Galatians 5:13 - "You, my brothers and sisters, were called to be free. But do not use your freedom to indulge the flesh; rather, serve one another humbly in love."

CONSIDER "SERVING FROM YOUR OVERFLOW" – SERVING OTHERS FROM A PLACE OF ABUNDANCE RATHER THAN OBLIGATION. HOW CAN YOU CULTIVATE A LIFE THAT ALLOWS YOU TO SERVE IN THIS WAY?

FREE SPACE

CHAPTER TAKEAWAYS

Date:

STEPPING INTO JOYIONAIRE STATUS

As we turn the pages to this final chapter, we find ourselves at a pivotal juncture in our journey towards joy. Here, the essence of all we have discovered about ourselves converges, inviting us to step into a life where joy is not just an occasional visitor but a steadfast companion. This chapter is a celebration of your transformation, a recognition of the depths you've explored, the truths you've embraced, and the growth you've nurtured. You are now ready to claim your "Joyionaire Status," walking confidently in the abundance of joy that is inherently yours. Embrace this moment as your own, where every lesson learned and every challenge overcome has led you to this point of unwavering joy. Welcome to your new beginning, where your life is rich with contentment, gratitude, and the profound beauty of simply being.

Romans 15:13 - "May the God of hope fill you with all joy and peace as you trust in him, so that you may overflow with hope by the power of the Holy Spirit."

DEFINE WHAT BEING A "JOYIONAIRE" MEANS TO YOU. HOW DOES THIS VISION INFLUENCE YOUR DECISIONS AND DIRECTION IN LIFE?

Romans 15:13 - "May the God of hope fill you with all joy and peace as you trust in him, so that you may overflow with hope by the power of the Holy Spirit."

REFLECT ON THE JOURNEY OF SHEDDING POUNDS (PHYSICAL, EMOTIONAL, SPIRITUAL) TO GAIN PURPOSE. WHAT WAS A PIVOTAL MOMENT IN THIS JOURNEY FOR YOU?

Romans 15:13 - "May the God of hope fill you with all joy and peace as you trust in him, so that you may overflow with hope by the power of the Holy Spirit."

JOYIONAIRES OFTEN INSPIRE OTHERS. SHARE HOW YOU PLAN TO USE YOUR STORY AND EXPERIENCES TO EMPOWER THOSE AROUND YOU.

Romans 15:13 - "May the God of hope fill you with all joy and peace as you trust in him, so that you may overflow with hope by the power of the Holy Spirit."

BEING A JOYIONAIRE IS AS MUCH ABOUT RECEIVING AS IT IS ABOUT GIVING. DESCRIBE A MOMENT WHEN RECEIVING JOY FROM OTHERS TRANSFORMED YOUR OUTLOOK.

Romans 15:13 - "May the God of hope fill you with all joy and peace as you trust in him, so that you may overflow with hope by the power of the Holy Spirit."

LOOKING FORWARD, WHAT ARE THREE GOALS YOU HAVE FOR YOUR CONTINUED JOURNEY AS A JOYIONAIRE? HOW DO THESE GOALS REFLECT YOUR GROWTH AND ASPIRATIONS?

FREE SPACE

CHAPTER TAKEAWAYS

Date:

Comprehensive Checklist for Spiritual Wellness

Rate each statement based on your recent feelings and behaviors. Circle your number 1(rarely) to 5(always)

Daily Spiritual Practices:

Have my practices deepened or become more meaningful?   1   2   3   4   5

Am I exploring different forms of spiritual expressions or sticking to what's familiar?   1   2   3   4   5

Mindfulness and Emotional Regulation:

How well do I manage stress through spiritual techniques?   1   2   3   4   5

Am I better at controlling impulses and managing reactions?   1   2   3   4   5

Gratitude and Positive Outlook:

How has my perspective on life's challenges changed?   1   2   3   4   5

Am I able to see difficult situations as opportunities for growth?   1   2   3   4   5

Community and Service:

How have my interactions contributed to my spiritual growth?   1   2   3   4   5

Am I involved in any service activities that align with my spiritual values?   1   2   3   4   5

Comprehensive Checklist for Spiritual Wellness

Rate each statement based on your recent feelings and behaviors. Circle your number 1(rarely) to 5(always)

Learning and Adaptability:

Am I open to new spiritual ideas and teachings?

1   2   3   4   5

How often do I seek out and engage with new spiritual knowledge and practices?

1   2   3   4   5

Personal Reflection and Integrity:

How consistently do I live out my spiritual beliefs in daily actions?

1   2   3   4   5

Am I more aligned with my core values and principles than before?

1   2   3   4   5

REFLECTION

REFLECTION

30 DAYS OF GRATITUDE

Day 1		Day 16	
Day 2		Day 17	
Day 3		Day 18	
Day 4		Day 19	
Day 5		Day 20	
Day 6		Day 21	
Day 7		Day 22	
Day 8		Day 23	
Day 9		Day 24	
Day 10		Day 25	
Day 11		Day 26	
Day 12		Day 27	
Day 13		Day 28	
Day 14		Day 29	
Day 15		Day 30	

Thank you

Dear Joyionaire,

From the deepest reaches of my heart, thank you. By choosing this workbook, you've not only invested in your health and happiness but also in a journey towards a purpose-driven life. Your decision to embark on this path with me is not only brave but profoundly meaningful.

Your courage to face challenges head-on, your willingness to transform, and your faith in a brighter, joy-filled future are what make this journey so special. Each page you've turned, every reflection you've penned, and every goal you've set, have been steps towards not just achieving but living your purpose.

This workbook was born from my own trials and triumphs, crafted with the hope that my story would light a path for others. And here you are, proving that when we share our stories, we multiply our joys and divide our burdens. You've allowed me to be a part of your journey, and for that, I am incredibly grateful.

Remember, every day is a new opportunity for growth and joy. Keep pushing forward, keep reaching for your dreams, and most importantly, keep trusting in the transformative power of faith and action.

May your path be blessed with health, your life with joy, and your actions with purpose. With all my gratitude and blessings,

Caleb Jakes